Original title:

Feathers in the Mist

Author: Simon Fairchild

ISBN HARDBACK: 978-1-80586-201-7

ISBN PAPERBACK: 978-1-80586-673-2

Until the Dawn Breaks

The rooster dreams of breakfast goals,
Yet snores like lazy, sleepy holes.
Chickens cluck in pajamas bright,
As night debates with morning light.

The stars slip off their twinkly hats,
As rabbits bounce like rubber bats.
The moon trips over hills of cream,
In this oddball, wacky dream.

Amidst the Veil

A foggy dance of silly shades,
Where squirrels wear their masquerades.
They giggle, leap, and tease the trees,
With acorn hats that float like bees.

The lantern bugs take a bow so grand,
In a lighting show that's simply planned.
They waltz around with mouse-ball chains,
As laughter echoes, spreading gains.

The Last Caress of Light

The sun bows low, a silly clown,
With bulbous cheeks of golden brown.
It tickles clouds with beams so bright,
While shadows dance in sheer delight.

A cat in shades pulls off a stunt,
And all the daisies seem to flaunt.
With giggles caught in evening's sigh,
The night just yawns and says goodbye.

When Gossamer Meets the Ground

The spider hosts a costume ball,
With threads so fine they float and sprawl.
A butterfly forgets its shoes,
And ends up stuck in morning dew.

The mist rolls in with giddy flair,
While frogs turn poets in their lair.
Each lily pad becomes a stage,
As nature sings through every page.

Lurking Between Shadows

In the twilight, things take flight,
A clumsy squirrel gives a fright.
Chasing glimpses, slipping passed,
In shadows, laughs are unsurpassed.

A cat yawns wide in the night,
Wonders if it's a bird in flight.
But lo! It's just a swaying tree,
That dances with a mystery.

A Dance of Delicate Wings

In the garden, bugs do twirl,
With every flap, their colors swirl.
A butterfly slips, trips and squeaks,
While ladybugs climb up their cheeks.

Tiny wings on a wild spree,
Flipping here, then flying free.
They giggle as they sway and spin,
In this ballet, let the fun begin!

Veiled Echoes

Whispers tickle the midnight air,
As shadows play without a care.
A crow calls out with a hoot,
While mice beneath his feet do scoot.

A rustle here, a tumble there,
Excitement brews in the night's glare.
With every sound, a giddy chase,
In this sneaky, game-filled space.

Shrouded in Softness

A blanket of gray hugs the ground,
While giggles, oh, how they resound!
Hiding from shadows that softly loom,
As whispers rise in a fluffy plume.

With soft steps they bounce and sway,
Making mischief in a playful way.
Through huddled whispers, laughter glows,
In cozy corners, where joy flows.

The Weight of Misty Secrets

In the cloak of fog, I tripped on a cloud,
Tumbling and laughing, a little too loud.
Birds above giggled, they knew my plight,
Whispered my secrets in pure delight.

Invisible friends danced all around,
Wings on the breeze, they twirled and they bound.
I paused and I chuckled at shadows that swung,
Maybe they'll tell me what songs could be sung.

A ghostly parade with no one in sight,
I asked for their wisdom, they shrugged, "That's alright!"

Then one made a quip, oh so obscured,
I laughed and agreed, the wise merely blurred.

In this misty realm, I'm never alone,
With featherless jesters who just want to drone.
Secrets are funny, wrapped tight in a jest,
Under this shroud, we're all just a fest.

Glances of Hidden Beauty

I spotted a glimmer from under a vine,
A wink from the undergrowth, oh so divine.
A squirrel turned pink, with eyes made of glee,
As if sharing secrets, just him and me.

The trees leaned in close, with snickers galore,
"Watch out for puddles!" they laughed, "What a chore!"
But I leapt like a dancer, all grace till I fell,
And splashed with wild joy, in my mud-coated shell.

A rustle behind, was it love on the wing?
Or just a lost parrot that fancied to sing?
I told it, "Just strut, and don't fret over looks,
You shine much more brightly than those glossy books!"

In glances of mischief, beauty resides,
With each little laugh, like a chubby that glides.
Underneath all this humor, a charm we can glean,
In a world full of giggles, what more could we mean?

Muffled Songs of the Night

The stars giggle softly, their light made of lace,
While shadows debate about who wins the race.
A mouse in the moonlight sneezed with a whiff,
And startled the crickets, who could not quite sift.

Bats held a concert, a cacophony sweet,
With squeaks and with flutters, they boomed like a treat.
I clapped just a tad, for my audience small,
As night creatures crooned, and I toed the hall.

A cloud passed by, with a wink and a dance,
It twirled above me, inviting a chance.
"Come join our parade!" it whispered with cheer,
But I tripped over starlight and rolled like a deer!

They laughed all around, in this nonsensical play,
Where night holds its secrets, all whimsical sway.
Muffled songs intertwined like a dream I can share,
With giggles of magic that dance through the air.

Time's Tender Caress

Tick-tock went the clock, wearing a grin,
As sediment dusted the old violin.
Time played a prank, on that chair by the wall,
Where I tripped on a tale with no end at all.

A passage of giggles from years long ago,
Whispered in shadows, where memories flow.
"Dear child," it exclaimed, "just keep up the pace,
For life's a quick jester, with time to embrace!"

The hands of the clock spun some wild little tales,
Of silly misnomers and faint fairy trails.
"What if I danced?" I challenged the chime,
But landed right back, just a second behind!

Yet time wasn't harsh, it just chuckled away,
As I wrestled my shoes in a humorous fray.
In this tender caress, let the laughter be full,
For life's just a jest, so let's play the fool!

Migrating Shadows

A flock of quirks in clouds of gray,
They flap and giggle, float away.
With every quack, a silly dance,
They trip on air, a comic chance.

The sun hides laughter, smiles collide,
As shadows chase, they cannot hide.
They zig and zag in loops so wide,
In this funny game, they won't abide.

A silly tale beneath the mist,
With ruffled wings, they can't resist.
A squawk, a honk, oh what a sight,
In shadows they will play tonight.

So let them flit, mischievous band,
With cheeky grins, they take a stand.
When humor slips beneath the skies,
Migrating shadows bring surprise!

Whispers of Forgotten Times

In the attic dust where secrets creep,
Old relics chuckle, not a peep.
A reminder of mischief, lost to age,
They tickle memories, turn the page.

"What's that?" a tin can starts to bray,
"Didn't I dance in the grand ballet?"
With rusty hinges, laughs erupt,
As laughter flows, the past erupts.

Forgotten toys in corners hide,
With each tickle, they spring alive.
They bounce and wobble as stories renew,
In the whispers of laughter, they mimic the crew.

So gather round, those tales forlorn,
Bring forth the giggles, both night and morn.
For every shadow holds a jest,
In forgotten times, the fun's the best!

Windsong and Wonder

There's a breeze that hums a playful tune,
With tickling whispers beneath the moon.
It dances through branches, a spirited friend,
Gathering giggles with each little bend.

The leaves chuckle as they take flight,
Swirling in chaos, what a sight!
They rustle and rattle, a breezy jest,
In the windsong's arms, they find their nest.

A squirrel joins in, a jump and twirl,
He spins so fast, his cheeks in a whirl.
Chasing the breeze, they share a laugh,
As nature's jesters write a silly path.

So let the winds bring wonder near,
With every gust, we'll shed a tear.
Laughter floats on a zephyr's kiss,
In this playful breeze, we find our bliss!

Threads of the Unseen

In the loom of life, apparitions weave,
With tangled threads, they play and cleave.
A wink from a ghost, a tickle so sly,
In the fabric of laughter, they take to the sky.

"Catch me if you can!" a whisper sings,
As shadows twirl in imaginary rings.
They stretch and twist, a delightful spree,
In the dance of the unseen, we laugh with glee.

A tapestry bright, with colors unseen,
Threads of humor, crisp and keen.
Every snicker stitches a tale,
As the funny phantoms start to prevail.

So hold on tight as the laughter doth spin,
In the fabric of life, let the fun begin.
For in every thread, a jest does lie,
In the unseen realms, we soar and fly!

The Ephemeral Light of Dusk

In twilight's glow, a chicken pranced,
It danced and twirled, so oddly chanced,
With shadows creeping, giggles grew,
As it mistook the moon for a shoe.

A sheep ran by in polka-dot,
It leaped and bounced, a jolly lot,
With all its wool, it lost its way,
And thought the field was one big play.

The crickets chirped a silly tune,
While rabbits joined, beneath the moon,
They laughed aloud, a merry throng,
As dusk swept in with its playful song.

But night fell fast, with shadows long,
The chicken dreamed of a dance so strong,
And as it twirled, let out a peep,
While the world around it fell asleep.

Pilgrimage of the Wandering

A duck in boots walked down the lane,
With a map that showed a watery vein,
It quacked aloud, "Now where to go?"
But its reflection said, "Just take it slow."

The mice were in a tiny boat,
Sailing along, they'd freely float,
With tiny paddles, they splashed about,
While seagulls laughed, with a raucous shout.

A turtle joined, so very late,
It brought some snacks and said, "Just wait!"
With sandwiches made of leaves and cheese,
They feasted slow, beneath the trees.

Then off they went, a merry band,
With silly songs and dreams so grand,
In a world so full of quirks and fun,
Their pilgrimage had just begun.

Starlit Driftwood Dreams

A driftwood log had plans to fly,
It hoped to touch the starlit sky,
"Hang on tight," a raccoon said,
While munching snacks, not filled with dread.

The moon looked down and gave a wink,
As the pierogs danced on the brink,
A crab said, "Join, don't be a bore!"
While starfish clapped upon the shore.

With twinkling lights, a wacky crew,
The sea sang songs of a dream or two,
They twirled and spun, a jubilant sight,
Each hoping to win the cosmic flight.

Then dawn approached with golden rays,
But laughter lingered through their plays,
As driftwood dreams in starlit beams,
Gave way to joy, and silly schemes.

Secrets Beneath the Surface

In the garden, a squirrel does prance,
With a nut in its cheek, ready to dance.
The wind whispers secrets, oh so sly,
As leaves eavesdrop from way up high.

A rabbit jumps in, with a curious glance,
It hops around in its jiggly stance.
The earthworms are plotting, in secret delight,
While gnomes chill in shadows, avoiding the light.

Chasing shadows and twirling in fun,
Frogs croak their laughter, a chorus begun.
Forget all the worries, just let it flow,
For antics abound when the sun's in tow.

A parrot complains of the noise on the ground,
It's a wild little party when friends gather 'round.
With giggles and chuckles, we savor the chance,
To dance in the chaos, our own silly prance.

Thistle and Dew

Tiny droplets cling to leaves bright,
While bees buzz around in the morning light.
A thistle tickles, in jests it pokes,
As we stumble and giggle, surrounded by folks.

The roses complain, so prissy and proud,
But the sun's silly rays make them laugh loud.
With prickles and petals all mixed in a bunch,
We dance through the garden, a bright colorful punch.

The deer prance softly, with grace in each stride,
While hedgehogs roll over, with nothing to hide.
It's a frolicsome tale, a humorous sight,
In the thicket of laughter, pure joy taking flight.

Frogs leap over puddles, jumpy with cheer,
They croak tunes of nonsense for all to hear.
With thistle as witness to giggles and tease,
Nature's a jester, bringing smiles with ease.

Wisps of Aether

Up in the clouds, the balloon animals bounce,
Chasing the wind with a gleeful pounce.
A jester in yonder throws pies in the air,
While cotton candy unicorns flutter with flair.

The breeze whispers jokes only stars can get,
As owls hoot in giggles, their eyes a bright set.
Moonbeams are sparkling, winking in play,
While shadows do the cha-cha, come out to sway.

A flock of balloons floats around the sky,
With creatures of laughter that zip and fly.
They tickle the clouds, a whimsical crew,
Painting the ether with giggles anew.

The sun, with a chuckle, warms up the day,
Shining on nonsense, inviting the play.
Here in the twilight, where fun takes its course,
We'll dance with the wisps and ride on the horse.

Tapestry of Lost Colors

In the attic of dreams, where colors take flight,
A mishmash of canvas, oh what a sight!
Crayons conspire with brushes in hand,
As they chuckle and giggle, a colorful band.

A blue and a yellow collide with a thud,
Creating a squishy, delightful mud.
The red ones complain, feeling a spat,
While purple just laughs, curled up on a mat.

Canvases giggle at stumbles and slips,
As splatters of color dance on our lips.
With each stroke a story, each swirl a delight,
We weave a mad tapestry under moonlight.

The laughter of pigments paints joy in the air,
With chaos and giggles, we don't have a care.
In this whimsical world where colors can play,
We stitch together moments, in our funny way.

Glimmers of Vanishing Plumage

A chicken in a tutu, it struts with glee,
Chasing after whispers, wild and free.
Its friends all chuckle as it twirls around,
In a dance of chaos, laughter is found.

But where are the feathers? They've flown away,
Dancing with the breeze, they'd rather play.
The rooster crows, as it watches the fun,
Wishing for a feathered costume to run.

Yet here comes a sheep, with a grand disguise,
Sporting bright plumes that could win any prize.
They prance through the meadow, giggling with cheer,
Who knew farm antics could bring such a tear?

So let's raise a toast to the peacocks and hens,
Whose shimmering antics lead to endless grins.
For in this silly world, we find our delight,
In the mirth of the creatures taking flight.

Feathered Shadows on the Breeze

A parrot with sunglasses, perched on a post,
Sipping lemonade, it likes to boast.
Winging its way to the clouds up high,
Just a little too proud, oh my, oh my!

The duck in a bowtie trots near with flair,
Claiming to be the chicest creature out there.
With a waddle so dapper, it orders a drink,
While a chicken in heels gives us all time to think.

What a sight to see, such a funny parade,
With a rooster on drums, their talents displayed.
They dance on the grass, in the soft morning light,
Creating shadows giggling, oh what a sight!

So let's hum a tune to this feathered brigade,
Who fill every moment with joy and no shade.
In this quirky carnival, laughter's the prize,
As they flap through the day 'neath the blue, sunny skies.

Luminous Drift of Quiet Moments

A wise old owl perched in a tree,
Winks at the squirrels—what could they see?
A fox jumps up, wearing socks on its paws,
In the glow of twilight, deserving applause.

The rabbits all giggle in their fuzzy hats,
As the badger juggles with acorn-spiked bats.
In this whimsical world where laughter ignites,
Every quiet moment now twinkles with sights.

The fireflies twirl, drawing circles of light,
While the feathered brigade takes off in mid-flight.
A sing-songy chorus erupts from below,
As even the crickets join in on the show.

So let us enjoy this luminous drift,
Where every soft giggle can be a gift.
In the hush of the night, as hilarity swells,
Funny friendships blossom with delightful tales.

Veils of Feathered Light

On a swing made of feathers, a parakeet flies,
Looping through daisies, it reaches the skies.
With a splash of bright colors, it twirls with great glee,
Singing soft songs to the bright bumblebee.

A goat with a beret joins in for a ride,
As ducks in a line all paddle with pride.
They laugh all together, in a comedic plight,
In this world of pure whimsy, nothing feels right.

Each feather a secret, each laugh a delight,
Creating a tapestry echoing the night.
So dance with the shadows, let merriment sprout,
In a world spun with giggles, we all laugh out loud.

With the moon shining bright, let us revel and play,
With a chorus of chuckles, we brighten the day.
In this feathery wonderland, life feels just right,
Spinning of joy in the soft feathered light.

Chasing the Wind

There once was a cat with a hat,
Chasing breezes and looking quite fat.
He leaped and he spun,
Oh what silly fun,
As leaves danced around like a chat!

He swirled in the air, what a sight!
His friends joined the game with delight.
They twirled on the ground,
In laughter, they found,
The joy of the day's sheer delight!

Essence of Fleeting Clouds

A duck in a tutu flew high,
With a wink and a quack, oh so spry!
He wobbled a bit,
Was this all just wit?
Clouds giggled and echoed his cry!

The sun peeked through, gave a grin,
As the clouds swirled around with a spin.
They painted the blue,
With silly things too,
Like ice cream cones and a min!

The Enchantment of Solitude

In the quiet of twilight's soft glow,
A squirrel made friends with a crow.
They shared silly tales,
Of moonlit veils,
And danced like no one else would know!

But soon came a breeze, quite rude,
Knocking over their nuts, oh so crude!
With a laugh and a cheer,
They chased without fear,
In solitude, finding true mood!

A Tapestry of Whispers

A rabbit with shoes made of fluff,
Told stories so weird, yet so tough.
He hopped and he laughed,
All the woodland craft,
Echoing secrets, never enough!

With owls in the trees sharing jokes,
The bushes erupted with pokes.
A tapestry spun,
Of laughter and fun,
With each tiny whisper of folks!

Whirls of Delicate Patterns

In the air they dance and spin,
A flurry of colors now begins.
Like quirky socks with mismatched pairs,
They twirl around without a care.

Caught in wind's playful embrace,
They zigzag like a wandering grace.
A laugh erupts as one takes flight,
Turning moments into sheer delight.

Both soft and silly, a whimsical sight,
As they bounce along, oh what a flight!
They whisper secrets in breezy tones,
Tickling our hearts, like funny old bones.

So let them whirl, let them play,
Like jolly clouds that won't decay.
A riot of giggles in every sway,
A joyful memory at the end of the day.

Twilight's Soft Caress

As shadows stretch and giggles rise,
The evening slips with playful sighs.
Clouds play hide and seek with the sun,
Bringing rest and laughter, oh what fun!

Silly whispers flutter and tease,
As twilight dances with such ease.
Stars pop out in a sparkling jest,
In a lighthearted game, they're truly best.

A gentle breeze with a cheeky grin,
Tickles the night with a joyful spin.
Pigeons coo in their silly way,
Making mischief till break of day.

Like children sneaking out for fun,
Twilight brings giggles, the day is done.
In this quiet romp, we find our place,
Under the stars with a cheerful face.

The Remnants of Flight

Leftover giggles float through the air,
As wanderers wander without a care.
Traces of laughter, a feather or two,
Scribbles of joy in the sky's bright blue.

Squawking like ducks, the antics unfold,
Chasing their shadows, so bright and bold.
The whimsy of wings, a sight to see,
As they jaunt through the clouds, wild and free.

In puddles that shimmer, their echoes remain,
Each ripple a joke, a soft playful gain.
Catching the wind like a playful grin,
With snippets of joy as adventures begin.

So here's to the paths little hearts trace,
In the remnants of laughter, there's always a space.
For chuckles and chuckles, let's toast to good cheer,
As the remnants of flight bring us all near.

Serene Moments Unfold

In quiet corners, a giggle hides,
Serene moments where joy abides.
Little whispers brush against the trees,
Sending ripples of laughter in each gentle breeze.

Unexpected hiccups make us pause,
In serene depths, we laugh because.
A squirrel spins tales of wild mischief,
Making every mundane moment a gift!

With sun-kissed warmth, we gather around,
As merriment blooms in every sound.
Smiles exchange like the sweetest prize,
In fleeting encounters, where laughter lies.

So cherish those moments, unique and rare,
As serene happiness floats in the air.
With grins that stretch from ear to ear,
In the stillness, let joy persevere.

Chimeras in Flight

A bird flew by with socks so bold,
It looked quite silly, a sight to behold.
With each flap, it wobbled and swayed,
Who knew socks could make feathers parayed?

A creature danced without a care,
In rainbow hues, it filled the air.
It laughed and darted, oh what a sight,
Chasing butterflies, just out of spite!

A frog joined in, wearing a tie,
Singing loud while forgetting to fly.
The sky became a circus show,
As chimeras waltzed, putting on a glow.

In this wild flight, no one seems lost,
Joy is found in the oddest cost.
With giggles and guffaws, they chase the dawn,
In this whimsical world, all worries are gone.

The Stillness of Breathing Wings

A turkey sat on a branch so stout,
Dreaming of flight, it gave a shout.
"Where's my jet pack? Where's my speed?"
Its dreams of soaring made others plead.

Squirrels chuckled from their high top trees,
"Try gliding down; it's much like a breeze!"
But the turkey puffed up, full of despair,
"Gliding is for folks without any flair!"

Little did it know, as it plotted and schemed,
That sometimes the ground is all that it dreamed.
It clucked and fluffed, thinking, "I'm grand!"
Underneath its dreams, it sank in the sand.

Despite the stillness, laughter took flight,
As friends gathered 'round to revel in sight.
And though it couldn't soar or swing,
The joy was enough for the stillness of wings.

Music of the Fading Day

The sun dips low, the crickets start,
As shadows dance, playing their part.
A chorus of chirps and a giggle of breeze,
Compose an evening, bringing us ease.

A snail croons softly into the dark,
While a raccoon taps, creating a spark.
Join in the jive, let your spirit sway,
In this concert of dusk, we play and play!

The wind blows strong, like a trumpet's blare,
Mice on tiny drums fill up the air.
A dandelion floats, flirting with fate,
As night draws near, we dance with a gait.

So let's sway with humor till stars do grace,
For laughter lingers in this cozy space.
Though the day is fading, the fun won't sway,
In the music of twilight, we all find our way.

Phantoms in the Twilight

As shadows blend with the evening light,
A ghost of a chicken gives quite a fright.
It tiptoes softly with pot on head,
In search of the corn that lies up ahead.

Hoots of an owl join in the fun,
As spooks start dancing, one by one.
"Who's got the popcorn?" a phantom did cheer,
"Just a ghoulish snack that we all hold dear!"

The wind starts to play, a haunting tune,
While cackling spirits make mischief soon.
"Let's play hide and seek, it's almost night!"
Who'd ever think ghosts could be so polite?

In this twilight dance, we giggle and sway,
With friends from the past who longed to play.
So haunt us sweetly, spooks of delight,
For laughter and whimsy spark up the night.

Ephemeral Glimmers

In the twilight, things take flight,
A chicken winks at a kite bright.
Squirrels giggle in a race,
As the moon wears a silly face.

Whispers dance on evening air,
While cats perform without a care.
A duck wears socks upon its feet,
The town can't help but laugh with glee.

Balloons escape with a cheerful pop,
While pigeons take a twirl and hop.
Stars peer down with a jest,
Cosmic tricks put life to the test.

In the shadows, gnomes conspire,
To steal away the evening's fire.
Every giggle echoes wide,
In this absurdity, we abide.

The Aerial Embrace

Crows perform acrobatics bold,
While owls exchange tales of old.
A squirrel slides on a windy breeze,
Tickling leaves on giggling trees.

Atop the world, a chicken sings,
Claiming the sky's most regal things.
A canvas painted with laughter bright,
As clouds wear hats in pure delight.

Rabbits hop with a joyful cheer,
Pirouetting with nary a fear.
The sun winks at the playful breeze,
Nature's jesters dance with ease.

A butterfly cracks a silly joke,
Leaves shake in laughter; what a hoax!
In this ballet of the sky's grace,
Laughter thrives in every space.

Secrets of the Pale Sky

Under the cloak of moonlight's gleam,
A cat reveals its quirky dream.
Stars giggle, twinkling bright,
While clouds play peek-a-boo with night.

Dandelions spin in a funny whirl,
As fireflies float, a luminous swirl.
A frog dons glasses, quite the sight,
Croaking sonnets in sheer delight.

The wind tells tales of playful sprites,
While owls doze in feathered nights.
A rabbit slips on a banana peel,
Its laughter is what we all feel.

The horizon blushes, a vibrant tease,
As the stars waltz with the gentle breeze.
Secrets linger, whispers play,
In this comedy of the night and day.

Fleeting Moments of Grace

We find joy in the swish of tails,
As raccoons plot their tricky trails.
A parrot jokes, "Why did you flee?"
"I'm just here for the comedy!"

Sunset dips like a clown in paint,
While kittens roll; oh, how quaint!
Butterflies chat on flimsy air,
Paws behind them, a little bear.

The breeze brings whispers, laughter's song,
Nature's circus, where we belong.
A goat dances on the fence's edge,
Declaring freedom is its pledge.

In the twilight, humor blooms,
As shadows wiggle in tiny rooms.
Life's a jest, trapped in a chase,
In these fleeting moments of grace.

Clouded Lullabies

In the fog, the giggles play,
Little birds have lost their way.
They dance around and flap their wings,
Singing tunes of silly things.

Hats on heads, they twirl about,
Chasing shadows, there's no doubt.
The clouds above just shake with glee,
As they join in the mystery.

A penguin slides, a rabbit hops,
While mucking up the misty drops.
A wobbly duck in fuzzy socks,
Grins wide, with laughter it unlocks.

So let the fog provide the stage,
For antics wild that never age.
In this cloudy, funny scene,
Happiness reigns, like a dream!

Elusive Hymns

A choir sings in muffled tones,
Among the gnomes and playful bones.
They wear their hats all askew,
In the mist, who knows what's true?

Chirps and squeaks flutter about,
As quirky critters dance and shout.
The notes are high, the beats are low,
Fuzzy ghosts steal the show!

A cat in a cloak, sleek and sly,
Winks at the crows that swoop and fly.
With every twist, the echoes play,
In this foggy ballet, hooray!

Their laughter rings, a playful tune,
Bouncing off the clouds like a balloon.
Join the fun, don't miss a chance,
To dance with them in this silly prance!

Ethereal Shadows Among Us

Ghostly forms in silly shapes,
Popping out with goofy capes.
They tickle feet and pull your hair,
With whispers floating through the air.

A wink from one, a giggle from two,
"Bet you can't catch me!" they coo.
Around the trees and through the grass,
They tumble, roll, and play en masse.

Missing socks and mismatched shoes,
These pesky spirits spread the news.
That laughter's better in the haze,
Where every day feels like a maze.

Let's follow them, oh what a chase!
In the fog, we find our place.
With shadows dancing all around,
We'll laugh and hop, where joy is found!

Threaded with Ghosts

In the weave of day's soft loom,
Threaded spirits share the room.
With puns and jests they gently tease,
In this mist, there's much to please.

A sock that dances, a hat that grins,
The whispers start as the fun begins.
"Why did the fog cross the street?" it sighs,
"To hug the clouds, oh what a surprise!"

Pinch of laughter, dash of cheer,
The friendly hauntings draw us near.
With every joke on tiptoes told,
These funny tales are purest gold.

Together, let's unravel this joy,
In misty realms we all enjoy.
So come along, don't be a ghost,
Join in the laughter, that's what matters most!

Murmurs of Celestial Down

In a world where birds don capes,
They waddle and dance like little apes.
With laughter their wings quiver and sway,
Creating a circus in the skies of gray.

Pigeons wear sunglasses, chic and bold,
While a robin juggles acorns, uncontrolled.
The crows plot pranks in secret huddles,
As seagulls lose bets in silly puddles.

Up above, the stars begin to chime,
A chorus of giggles, oh so sublime.
Sparrows recite poems in high-pitched rhymes,
Echoing joy, transcending all times.

A feather on a breeze spins round and round,
The softest whispers of a sweet sound.
But beware of the owl's trickster eyes,
For humor is hidden in laughter's disguise.

A Veil of Aviary Secrets

In a secret garden where sparrows dine,
With tiny top hats looking quite divine.
They flip-flop and tumble in playful fits,
Chasing each other, forming little skits.

A parrot in a wig tells jokes galore,
While the doves on swings ask for more.
A crow commissions a comedy show,
With punchlines that maytake time to grow.

Among the bushes, laughter erupts,
As drakes and hens in quirks interrupt.
They waddle in rhythm, a chubby parade,
With giggles that weave through lilies in shade.

Under moonlit skies, their secrets float,
A symphony of chuckles, a feathered anecdote.
With every flap and flirt, they weave delight,
Crafting a bonheur, a joyous night.

Serendipity in the Fog

In the misty veil where shadows play,
A duck slips and slides, finding her way.
With a quack that prompts a giggle or two,
Who knew ducks could frolic like me and you?

A startled owl hoots, losing her grace,
While pigeons wear hats, strutting in place.
Laughter rings out through the damp, cool air,
As sparrows join in with nibbles to share.

Under swirling clouds, they dance all about,
Creating a ruckus, they're free of doubt.
In the fog's embrace, all worries are tossed,
For laughter in the air makes the day less lost.

When mist wraps around them, and night starts to greet,
They spread joy like a blanket, soft and neat.
With a chuckle, they flitter, like sparks they ignite,
A whimsical world where humor takes flight.

Silken Threads of Flight

With a whoosh and a flutter, they rise to the night,
Balloons on a breeze in a fanciful flight.
A finch wears pajamas, so cozy and warm,
While swallows engage in a comical charm.

A goose with a megaphone starts a parade,
While a hen calls the shots, unafraid.
They giggle and squawk, causing quite a scene,
Cartwheeling through grasses, lively and keen.

As the moon draws a smile on each gleeful face,
A chorus of chirps fills the silken space.
With chuckles a-plenty, they flit and they play,
In a world of mischief, as colors sway.

So raise a toast to the birds on the rise,
With comedy woven through skies and goodbyes.
In their playful realm, the joy is complete,
With every sharp turn, they keep up the beat.

The Breath of Celestial Tides

A waddle of ducks breaks the dawn,
Their quacks echo loud, as if drawn.
They dance in the fog, oh what a sight,
Wings flapping wildly, a hilarious flight.

Down by the lake, a splash and a dive,
A frog joins the fun, so sly and alive.
He jumps amidst giggles, in tones of delight,
While the ducks make a ruckus, oh what a night!

A breeze carries laughter, soft and light,
As turtles roll over, not ready for flight.
The sun peeks through, with a wink in its rays,
Making all furry friends dance in a daze.

With each little ripple, a joke is told,
Nature's own comedy, a treasure to hold.
In this misty world where silliness flows,
Life is a show, and laughter just grows.

Misty Reveries

In the morning haze, a cat on a fence,
Paws misplaced, it sways, oh so intense.
A bird sings a tune that's slightly off-key,
The cat gives a glare, 'Hey, that's not for me!'

Beneath the tree branches, shadows twist and twine,
A squirrel takes cover, though it's ten past nine.
With acorns for props, he juggles with flair,
While the dog just watches, with a puzzled stare.

A rabbit hops by, wiggling its nose,
In the middle of the stage, a playful pose.
The audience giggles as it shows off its tricks,
As birds in the choir perform feathered flicks.

Oh, what a scene where laughter unfolds,
In dreamy adventures, no one grows old.
Misty mornings hold secrets of cheer,
Where whimsy and giggles are all that we hear.

Soft Enigmas

A misty swirl, a secret parade,
Chickens in hats, wearing their trade.
They strut with sass, clucking a tune,
When the rooster joins in, it's a midnight croon.

On the fence post, wise owls confer,
With spectacles perched, 'What's causing the blur?'
They squint and they ponder, with feathers so neat,
While a laughing crow offers them something to eat.

In the fog-drenched garden, a snail takes a crawl,
Waving hello to the worm at the wall.
Together they giggle, in slow-motion style,
As a butterfly flutters by in a while.

These soft enigmas, so curious and bright,
Bring laughter to mornings, from day into night.
For in this strange world where silliness reigns,
Each critter and creature knows joy that remains.

The Chorus of the Feathered

A silly goose leads the morning's choir,
With a honk as a note, a tune to inspire.
The sparrows gap-jaw, all fluff and all fuss,
In their little costumes, they gather with us.

A peacock struts by, all shiny and grand,
Winking at pigeons who shake their small bands.
Together they whistle, a riotous charm,
Every flap and flutter brings giggles, no harm.

The robins and finches join in on the prank,
With a dance on the branches, a colorful flank.
Who knew that the woods had such vibrant tunes?
As laughter resounds beneath smiling moons.

So let's raise a cheer for this feathered brigade,
Who share in the fun and make merriment parade.
In the echoes of morning, let silliness fly,
From each quack and chirp, to the burst in the sky.

Charmed by the Fog

In the haze, a duck takes flight,
Looking lost, what a sight!
With bread crumbs tossed in glee,
A banquet for birds, oh that'd be!

Sneaky squirrels, they sneak and creep,
As morning fog makes pathways deep.
A worm peeks up but slips away,
A tangled dance in disarray!

An owl hoots, unsure of his aim,
In this mist, it's all a game.
A giggle from the trees sounds bright,
Nature's laughter fills the night!

So here we are, with chuckles high,
In fog so thick, we almost fly.
Join the fun, and leap with zest,
In this misty, silly quest!

Surrender to the Breeze

A tumbleweed stole my hat,
Rolling on, just like that!
The wind howled with a teasing grin,
As I chased it, my socks wore thin.

A balloon floats, lost in the air,
A squirrel waves from his comfy chair.
The kites above dance with delight,
While I chase shadows, oh what a sight!

A paper plane drifts by with style,
Winking at me for a while.
I trip on my shoelace, laugh loud,
As the breeze cheers, feels like a crowd!

With giggles riding on the air,
I surrender—what a wild affair!
Let's frolic and play, swirl with the tease,
In this airy joy, let's all feel pleased!

The Ephemeral Hour

Time slips by on puffball clouds,
Tickling faces, drawing crowds.
As clocks tick backwards, wouldn't that be fun?
Maybe we'd dance until we're done!

Tea cups spin like merry-go-rounds,
Schrödinger cats study their bounds.
A brief moment, but oh, how it gleams,
Laughter spills like melting dreams.

Caught in whimsy, we might fall,
Into a giggling game, a free-for-all.
We chase the seconds, giggle and sway,
Let's absorb joy until it fades away!

So let's embrace the fleeting time,
With silly verses and playful rhyme.
For in this hour, wild and bright,
We're the jesters, taking flight!

Enigma of the Colors

In the garden where chaos breeds,
Purple tomatoes and yellow weeds.
A rainbow sneezed, it turned to gray,
And chuckled, "What a silly day!"

A bluebird croons a polka tune,
While lollipops grow beneath the moon.
With paintbrushes, we boldly dance,
Creating a world of fanciful chance.

A potted plant now wears a crown,
As marching ants parade around town.
The sun shines bright, then starts to chuckle,
As daisies don oversized buckles!

In colors wild, we swirl and spin,
Mixing giggles with the whimsy within.
Let's wrap this day in laughter's embrace,
In this enigmatic, painted space!

Whispers of Forgotten Wings

In the park, a pigeon struts,
With swagger like a king in ruts.
He fluffs his feathers, takes a bow,
While squirrels giggle, 'What a cow!'

A goose with style, he honks a tune,
As ducks tap dance beneath the moon.
A crowd forms round, they cheer and clap,
While rodents plot from their grass nap.

One bird lands atop a lopsided seat,
Declares, 'I rule this funny feat!'
But slips and flops down, what a sight,
Now they all burst out in pure delight.

With laughter filling the whole scene,
The feathered court with royal sheen,
In whimsies shared, their joy takes flight,
As giggles fill the starry night.

Shadows of Dappled Dreams

A crow in shades of twilight grins,
As cat below plots all her sins.
With leaps and bounds, she makes a mess,
That crow just caws, 'Oh, what a stress!'

A rustle comes from leafy boughs,
The raccoon peeks, then takes a bow.
But with one paw, he slips and slides,
While critters gain some extra rides.

A bunny hops in silly haste,
Chasing shadows, oh, what a race!
He trips and tumbles, rolls on the floor,
While all his friends just beg for more.

The sun dips low, they start to sway,
With laughter loud at end of day.
In woodland antics, hearts collide,
As silly shadows waltz and glide.

Echoes Beneath the Canopy

Beneath the branches, birds do squawk,
With clucks and caws, they seem to talk.
The parrot jokes, 'Who needs to sing?'
While mockingbirds weave tales in fling.

They share the tales of silly lore,
Of owls that wear a tutu score.
A turtle laughs, 'Oh, what a sight!'
As birds take flight with goofy might.

Then comes a jay with jarring song,
Declares, 'I've been cool all along!'
But in a blink, it trips and flops,
And all the forest belly drops.

In echoes loud beneath green leaves,
The laughter spreads as daylight weaves.
With creatures bold and stories spun,
Their joy cascades, a day well done.

Soft Plumage Adrift

A duckling wobbles near the stream,
With antics ripe for a good meme.
It flaps and flops, a clumsy flight,
While friends all cheer, 'You'll be alright!'

A pigeon perches with a smirk,
Claims to be the lord of work.
When crumbs are tossed, he dives with glee,
And lands headfirst, 'Oh, woe is me!'

The geese parade in perfect line,
Yet one gets lost, 'Oh, how divine!'
It honks and flaps in pure despair,
While others take the time to stare.

At dusk they gather, tales unwind,
With softest plumes and hearts entwined.
In jovial squawks, their laughter stays,
From silly moments birthed from plays.

A Dance of Spirit and Silence

In a grove where shadows play,
The whispers dance and skip away.
A wobbly sprite, with shoes too tight,
Trip over daisies, what a sight!

Giggles float on breezy wings,
They try to learn the silliest things.
With topsy-turvy, spin they sway,
While squirrels cheer and laugh, hooray!

Around the trees, they twirl and glide,
Invisible creatures take great pride.
They flounce and flop, a merry crew,
Creating mischief, just for you!

Such revelry within the glade,
Of sprightly misfits, unafraid.
A hush of laughter, soft delight,
As twilight brings the end of night.

The Elegance of Hidden Flight

Above the rooftops, zooms a blip,
A fizzy bird on a soda trip.
With wings like umbrellas, wild and wide,
It slips and slides with comical pride.

Pigeons glare with a haughty glance,
While this dorky fowl takes a chance.
It loops and flutters, then takes a dive,
Like a pop star on a live jive!

The crowd of critters starts to cheer,
As the vertigo turns to a leer.
With wobbly grace, it lands all wrong,
And joins the party with a silly song!

Oh, how the laughter fills the air,
In a flurry, they gather, none could compare.
Each flubbed landing a comedy gold,
In this sky of chaos, tales unfold.

Elysian Layers Above the Ground

Breezes tickle the kites up high,
While chubby squirrels attempt to fly.
A cloud of laughter, light and bright,
Panels of fluff in comical sight.

A robin's ballet stumbles and falls,
It lands on a cat, who gives stern calls.
The cat, bewildered, takes a leap,
While the robin giggles, not a peep!

In layers of cheer, the sky unzips,
As acorns tumble, here comes the flips.
Woodpeckers drum a silly tune,
Making mischief by afternoon.

Each flutter brings a burst of play,
As shadows chase the sunny ray.
Among the heights, where mischief flows,
Crazy laughter in every pose!

Traces of Grace in the Air

In a world where bubbles float,
An owl dons glasses, looks like a goat.
With every flap, it preens its feathers,
But lands on a fish—now that's rich treasure!

The giggling winds begin to whirl,
Chasing the clouds in a zany swirl.
As moths parade in whimsical flair,
Turning heads, they dance with flair.

Butterflies sporting shoes all wrong,
Trying to bust a move, oh so strong.
With each tumble and uneven twirl,
They cause a ruckus, a flappy whirl!

In skies where hilarity takes its place,
Round and round, what a funny chase.
These silly souls with a wink and grin,
Leaving trails of laughter in the wind!

Silent Conversations

In a world where ducks wear hats,
They quack in whispers, silly chats.
A pigeon struts, a peacock sighs,
With feathered friends, the gossip flies.

A crow in shades, so suave and neat,
Tells funny tales about a treat.
A squirrel eavesdrops with a grin,
While squirrels spin tales of acorn kin.

They gossip 'bout the silly crow,
Who thought he'd dance, but missed the show.
A duck fell down, lost in a tale,
While ospreys mapped the next big sale.

So here we are, with laughs abound,
In woodland talks, confusion found.
With silly secrets shared at dawn,
In this wild world, we carry on.

The Poetry of Flight

A bird in blue does twists and turns,
While talking trees share what it learns.
With every flap, a laugh is spread,
As clouds below shake their fluffy heads.

A parakeet recites a rhyme,
That makes the owls chuckle in time.
A hawk jokes, 'I'm a sight so grand,
But can't find my socks, isn't that grand?'

Through playful winds, the sparrows glide,
In search of snacks, they laugh, and slide.
With tales of mischief swirling near,
They paint the sky with giggles clear.

The art of flight, a funny show,
With air-bound pranks, and jokes in tow.
So as they soar, we can't resist,
The humorous dance of their twisty tryst.

Shadows Beyond the Horizon

At dusk when shadows start to play,
The echoes of birds lead the way.
A goose with dreams of being a star,
Flips through the clouds, saying 'Look, there's a car!'

The owls in huddles share their views,
On why the raccoons wear bright shoes.
A chatty bluejay tells a joke,
Of how a bear tried to ride a cloak.

Then comes the laugh of a dry-eyed crow,
Who lost a bet with a sly old doe.
They talk of antics far and wide,
With shadows giggling by their side.

In twilight's grip, they all convene,
And raucously laugh at the unseen.
So on this night, as dreams unwind,
The silliness roams, laughter entwined.

Layers of the Unfamiliar

In layers thick, the birds take flight,
With silly hats, a comical sight.
A sparrow tips his cap with grace,
Daring the robin to join the race.

They dive and twist, in antics grand,
As the sun dangles above, unplanned.
A vulture yawns, 'This game's a bust,'
While a college crow hones in on trust.

'What's your plan?' asks a wise old wit,
As a goose prepares a comedic skit.
With parachute dreams and noodle necks,
In this feathered world, joy connects.

So step with me through colors bright,
Where birds don shades and dance in sight.
Among the layers, laughter swells,
In the quirkiest tales that nature tells.

Enwrapped in Whispers

A gaggle of giggles hovers near,
Dreamy tales spun, loud and clear.
Ticklish secrets float in the air,
Eavesdroppers laugh but don't dare to share.

Wings of chatter dance on the breeze,
Playing hide and seek among the trees.
Every flutter holds a quirk or two,
Mystery wrapped in a splash of hue.

Forgetful ghosts with jokes to tell,
Drifting lightly, they cast a spell.
Tickles and snorts in a swirling din,
Grinning capers, let the fun begin!

As shadows stretch on the grassy floor,
Whimsical whispers keep wanting more.
In this light-hearted realm, we play,
Chasing laughter at the end of the day.

Ethereal Cargo

Above the world, they rise and fall,
Carrying giggles; can you hear the call?
Bouncing along on breezy arcs,
Laughter bottles, swirling sparks.

They stumble and fumble in mid-flight,
Spilling mayhem, a pure delight.
With every twist, a chuckle erupts,
As silly antics fill the interrupt.

Cargo of whimsy floats like a song,
Swerving left, and right, can't go wrong.
Tickled by breezes, they twist and spin,
How many spins 'til we fall in?

When night whispers softly, don't be shy,
Join the dance beneath the vast sky.
For even the stars can't resist the tease,
Of laughter spinning with humorous ease.

The Gentle Drift

Curious lightness carries the day,
Silly moments just drift away.
Capsizing thoughts on whimsy's stream,
Chasing chuckles, a daydream team.

With every breeze, a relaxed surprise,
Jokes bounce higher, oh how they rise!
Bouncing bubbles, laughter in tow,
Riding on currents, they sway to and fro.

Each drift brings a giggle, a snort,
Comical tales in a light-hearted sport.
Riddled with quirks, their mischief is sweet,
Can't help but dance to the mischievous beat.

As shadows stretch, the fun grows bold,
Witty whispers in stories retold.
In this lighthearted flight we dare,
To giggle, to gawk, and breathe in the air.

Celestial Curiosities

Up above, the stars all prance,
Giggling softly in a mischievous dance.
Wonders flutter on cosmic strings,
Quirky dreams in starlit flings.

Joking constellations in the night,
Winking down in sheer delight.
They twirl and swirl, a galactic tease,
Tickling wishes carried on the breeze.

Each comet's tail has a tale to share,
A funny story from up in the air.
With beams of laughter painting the sky,
Asteroids chuckle as they float by.

So dance with the stars and join their jest,
These celestial fools know how to best.
In a universe where silliness reigns,
Join the play where laughter remains.

Clouded Serenity

A chicken once dreamed of the skies,
But tripped on its own two thighs.
It flapped and it flailed, oh what a sight,
It ended up in a tree, what a fright!

The clouds giggled, with tails like kites,
As the chicken squawked, its best clumsy fights.
It squawked at the sun, quite out of line,
"I'm a bird!" it declared, while sipping on brine.

Its friends gathered round, full of delight,
"Just stick to the ground, don't take to flight!"
But off went the chicken, with hopes high above,
Only to land with a slap, what a shove!

In a puddle it landed, now muddy and bold,
With a grin on its beak, it ruffled its gold.
"Next time I'll fly!" it vowed with a laugh,
But for now, it just splashed in the aftermath!

Wings of Twilight

A bat with a joke aimed to impress,
Said, "What's a bird's favorite dress?
It's the wing thing, I swear it's true!"
But all the owls just hooted, "Boo!"

The sun dipped low, painted skies so bright,
A gaggle of geese took off in flight.
"Watch out for clouds!" one goose said with glee,
"Last time we crashed, we lost all our tea!"

They soared through the air, a sight so absurd,
Synchronized flapping, not one was deterred.
With beaks painted red, and a dance quite absurd,
They laughed at their blunders; oh, what a herd!

As twilight approached, a sight quite divine,
A raccoon in shades said, "Now that is fine!
Next gig is at dusk, with snacks on the menu,
Just mind the bees, or they'll bother you too!"

Embracing the Unseen

A pigeon perched high on its throne,
Declared, "I can see what you've never known!"
But a sly little cat had other plans,
"Your secrets are biscuits, you're a bad man!"

Through alleys they fluttered, in chaos and cheer,
Chasing each other, no worries or fear.
"Catch me if you can!" the birdies would tease,
Until they collided, nestles in leaves!

The cat would then laugh, "Is this hide and seek?
You say you're the master, but you're just weak!"
With wings all a-jumble, and feathers askew,
"Let's do it again!" the cat meowed, "Just you!"

As dusk settled down, a truce was declared,
Both critters decided they actually cared.
With the moon beaming down, they chuckled and played,

In a world of their own, where friendships are made!

Hidden in the Haze

A rabbit in leaves thought it could hide,
Caught a glimpse of its tail; oh, what a ride!
It sneezed with a hop, then out sprang a dash,
As the foggy night giggled, "What a big splash!"

The night critters chuckled, saw all the jest,
A badger remarked, "That's not how you nest!"
While fireflies blinked like they too had a plan,
To lead the lost bunny right out—oh, man!

"Follow my light!" one bright bug did say,
"While wearing that fluff, you'll scare me away!"
But the bunny just laughed, with a hop and a twirl,
"I'm the fluffiest thing, come join in my whirl!"

As the mist cleared away, what a sight it had been,
A whirl of fun critters, the night was a win.
With a toast to the fog, and a cheer loud and true,
They danced under stars; how silly they grew!

Embrace of the Untold

In shadows they gather, a whimsical crew,
With whispers of wonder, they plot and they stew.
A raucous parade of giggles and glee,
Invisible creatures, just take it from me.

A hat made of socks, the stylish attire,
They dance through the twilight, their spirits on fire.
A wink from the moon, a nudge from the night,
They twirl and they tumble, a comical sight.

With mashed-up confetti and sprouts on their heads,
They cast silly shadows on all of our beds.
Each chuckle, a spell, in the cool evening air,
Laughter's embrace, with nary a care.

In the end, they disperse like a bowl full of stew,
Leaving trails of giggles that dance as they flew.
So if ever you wonder what secrets abound,
Just listen for laughter, it's joy that's still found.

Chorus in the Shroud

A choir of giggles from beyond the grey,
Their melody floats, then scuttles away.
Invisible cabaret, nimbly they prance,
With a hitch in their step, it's a tip-toe romance.

Juggling odd objects, from spoons to old shoes,
While juggling a riddle, they jump with their clues.
A symphony of chaos, oh what a delight,
As they sing out of tune, under starlit night.

A curious jabber of nonsense and sound,
As secretive mummers from lost worlds abound.
With banter and jest, the night turns to gold,
In this tapestry woven of stories retold.

When morning arrives with a yawning cheer,
You'll smile at the echoes that tickle your ear.
The shroud disappears, as the sun starts to rise,
Leaving giggles adrift in the brightening skies.

The Secrets of the Skylark

A sky full of tricks, the skylark does weave,
With chirps that are riddles, you just can't believe.
She flits like a spark, with a wink and a grin,
As if nature herself is inviting you in.

A flurry of colors with twirls and a twist,
She dances through clouds, in a feathered mist.
With secrets she shares from high up on a beam,
Who knew little birds could contain such a dream?

Her songs are a puzzle, a riddle profound,
As giggles unwind and return to the ground.
The skylark, a jester, both crafty and sly,
Will tease you with echoes that soar through the sky.

So next time you're strolling where wild breezes dart,
Listen close for the secrets that dance in your heart.
For laughter is woven in all that she sings,
In the twisting of tales that each moment brings.

A Paradox of Softness

In a world made of fluff, the softest of beds,
Where clouds hold debates with imaginary heads.
The giggles are cozy, with warmth in the air,
Bouncing up and down in this light-hearted lair.

Paradoxes wrapped in a warm woolly coat,
Like sheep doing salsa, in shoes made of oat.
With no need for reason, just joy in the play,
They tumble through meadows at dawn of the day.

A tickle from daisies, they chuckle in glee,
As the butterflies flutter, a whimsical spree.
With each little bounce, and each giggle they share,
Their silliness dances in soft morning air.

So if you should wander where giggles expand,
Chase down the soft shadows that flit through the land.
For life's little parodies take flight with a grin,
In the fabric of laughter where magic begins.

Lines of the Invisible

A chicken struts, with flair so grand,
Wings spread wide, it takes a stand.
But oh! It trips and lands askew,
The crowd erupts, in laughter too.

The duck next door, so proud and spry,
Decides to soar, but oh my, oh my!
It flaps and flops with comical grace,
Finding itself in a noodle race.

A pigeon plans to take a leap,
Dreaming dreams all snug in sleep.
But when it wakes, it's in a spin,
Ruffled feathers, where to begin?

They float about on giddy trails,
Wobbling bumbles, flappy fails.
Together they dance, a silly sight,
In the morning breeze, oh what delight!

Tidal Currents of Air

The breeze came in, with playful jest,
As kites flew high, they passed the test.
One got tangled in a tree so wide,
Swinging about, it took a ride.

A seagull swooped to snatch a snack,
But missed the fries, it lost its track.
And with a squawk, it flapped away,
Stolen lunch turned to comedy play.

Twisting winds in a swirling dance,
Caught a squirrel in a breezy prance.
It leapt with gusto, a furball spree,
But never landed—not to be free.

As breezes blow and skies do twist,
The air is filled with laughs we missed.
So watch the skies, a funny show,
With each gust bringing whimsical woe!

The Weightless Dance

A flapping sock in a summer breeze,
Zigzagging wildly among the trees.
It sails so high, defies the ground,
As laughter wraps around the sound.

A paper plane took flight one day,
With dreams to soar, come what may.
But it hit a cat, who gave a look,
As if to say, "That's not in the book!"

A balloon skipped past on a sunny route,
Floating free—then it changed its snout.
With a loud pop, it fell in glee,
The giggles echoed from you to me.

When nothing weighs and joy is found,
The dance of air spins all around.
Float your worries, let laughter enhance,
Join the jovial, weightless dance!

Unknown Silhouettes

In the shadows where giggles hide,
Lies a chicken with swagger and pride.
It flutters near, with an awkward clap,
Making friends with a discarded wrap.

A squirrel darts by, not quite in view,
Scaling up walls, thinking it's new.
But it miscalculates, does a little twist,
And slides down fast—too funny to miss!

Behind the bush, a shadow peers,
A curious mole, full of silly fears.
It popped its head in, just for a peek,
Then dove away—what a sneaky sneak!

With laughter lurking where we can't see,
The silhouettes play, wild and free.
So join the whispers, the giggles, the fun,
In the dance of the unseen, everyone's won!

The Gossamer Path of Dreams

A bouncy cloud on a trampoline,
Floating high, feeling quite serene.
I wore my socks, but oh what luck,
Slipped and landed with a cluck!

Chasing shadows that dance around,
Stumbling softly, I trip and bound.
Laughter echoes in the twilight,
As I wipe off mud with all my might.

Cartwheels on a path of silver beams,
Twisting and turning on silly themes.
A butterfly whispers, 'Come and play!'
But I just tumble, what can I say?

In a world where giggles rule the air,
Every little stumble becomes a dare.
Wings of whimsy and joy collide,
In this frolicsome, dream-filled ride.

Enigmas in the Haze

The sun peeked through, a cheeky grin,
While squirrels plotted their next great win.
A riddle wrapped in a pancake's fluff,
Topped with syrup, oh so tough!

Clouds are hiding, playing a game,
They whisper secrets, but who's to blame?
I search for answers amidst the fog,
But end up juggling a lazy dog.

A pancake flipped and a cat that sings,
The morning giggles with such odd things.
Laughter bubbles in the misty gloom,
As I trip over an invisible broom!

Dancing shadows with giddy a sway,
Lost in a puzzle of sweet dismay.
They chuckle softly as I bewilder,
Trying to catch them, my mind's a whirler.

Secrets of the Morning Breeze

The wind carries whispers, oh so sly,
Like ducks in a row, they waddle by.
A chatty robin on a telephone line,
Tells the best jokes, it's such a sign!

With a whoosh and a swish, the trees confide,
While I try to sneak past, arms opened wide.
A squirrel giggles at my prancing feats,
It throws acorns, my head it beats!

Oh, the breeze tickles, it dances close,
Like a mischievous friend who likes to boast.
I chase the giggles that flutter and flit,
End up with mud, but isn't that a hit?

Every gust brings a chuckle or two,
Secrets in whispers, all fresh and new.
With laughter swirling in morning's air,
I twirl around without a care!

Celestial Echoes and Soft Glows

Stars wink down in a playful tease,
As moonlight chuckles, a gentle breeze.
I trip over stardust, what a sight,
End up laughing at the moon's delight.

Galaxies swirl like cotton candy spins,
And comet tails resemble silly grins.
Chasing fireflies, oh what a chase,
Each one giggles, it's a bright race!

Celestial echoes whisper out loud,
While I'm dancing with a cloud.
They tease my hair, a cosmic do,
With every swoop, I discover something new.

So here in the night, with twinkling glee,
Stars and silliness come out to see.
The universe giggles, it's all in fun,
As I pirouette under the bright, bold sun!